the Pursuit of Pleasure

Robert Rosenblum

Guggenheim Hermitage MUSEUM

Published on the occasion of the exhibition
The Pursuit of Pleasure
Guggenheim Hermitage Museum, Las Vegas
July 16, 2004–January 16, 2005
Organized by Susan Davidson, Arkady
Ippolitov, and Karl Schütz

ISBN 0-89207-319-5

Guggenheim Museum Publications
1071 Fifth Avenue
New York, New York 10128

Guggenheim Hermitage Museum
3355 Las Vegas Boulevard South
Las Vegas, Nevada 89109
www.guggenheimlasvegas.org

Design: Janice Lee, with Marcia Fardella
Production: Tracy L. Hennige
Editorial: Jennifer Knox White, Rachel
Shuman, and Edward Weisberger

Printed in Montreal by Transcontinental

Cover: detail of Louis Léopold Boilly,
A Game of Billiards, 1807 (cat. no. 22).

Contents

5   Directors' Statement

6   Acknowledgments

9   The Pursuit of Pleasure

CATALOGUE

15   Music and Dance

39   Celebration and Café Society

59   Gaming and Sport

83   Flirtation and Romance

Directors' Statement

The Pursuit of Pleasure is the fifth exhibition presented in Las Vegas at the Guggenheim Hermitage Museum and the second to recognize the unique alliance established in 2001 between the Solomon R. Guggenheim Foundation, New York, the State Hermitage Museum, St. Petersburg, and the Kunsthistorisches Museum, Vienna. This consortium of international institutions enables unprecedented intramuseum collaboration, including exhibitions, loan programs, Internet projects, publications, and educational outreach. The most rewarding result of our collaboration is the collection-sharing initiative that makes each institution's respective holdings available to broader audiences.

The Pursuit of Pleasure explores images of leisure in Western art from the sixteenth century to the early twentieth century. Throughout the centuries, the vocabulary of pleasure has been depicted in artworks in a variety of forms, from joy to delight, indulgence to amusement. Exploring these topics, the exhibition is organized into four sections—"Music and Dance," "Celebration and Café Society," "Gaming and Sport," and "Flirtation and Romance"—as represented by artists such as Max Beckmann, Marc Chagall, Edgar Degas, Jean-Honoré Fragonard, Pablo Picasso, Peter Paul Rubens, Jan Steen, Titian, Henri Toulouse-Lautrec, and Diego Rodríguez de Silva y Velázquez.

Not just subject matter, the pursuit of pleasure is inherent to the very nature of art itself through the sensory gratifications imparted to viewers: the rich qualities of color, shape, and texture and the implied sounds, smells, and tastes. Beyond this is the pleasure provided by the viewing of art as a shared activity. Here, the pursuit of pleasure is a crucial social function as well as a welcome visual indulgence. We invite you to enjoy *The Pursuit of Pleasure*, an exhibition realized specifically for a Las Vegas audience.

We would like to extend our appreciation to Susan Davidson, Curator at the Guggenheim, Arkady Ippolitov, Curator of Italian Prints at the Hermitage, and Karl Schütz, Director of the Gemäldegalerie at the Kunsthistorisches for their curatorial partnership, which began at the conception of the exhibition and has resulted in this dazzling achievement. Robert Rosenblum, Nan and Stephen Swid Curator of Twentieth-Century Art at the Guggenheim, has further delighted our readers with his deft and witty digressions on the pleasure received from looking at such masterpieces.

Thomas Krens
Director
Solomon R. Guggenheim Foundation

Mikhail Piotrovsky
Director
State Hermitage Museum

Wilfried Seipel
Director
Kunsthistorisches Museum

Acknowledgments

The Pursuit of Pleasure was first conceived in discussions with Thomas Krens, Director, and Lisa Dennison, Chief Curator and Deputy Director, Solomon R. Guggenheim Museum; Dr. Mikhail Piotrovsky, Director, State Hermitage Museum; and Wilfried Seipel, Director, Kunsthistorisches Museum, following the opening of the Guggenheim Hermitage Museum in the fall of 2001. We are grateful to them for their faith in this project and for the encouragement they have provided throughout.

In addition to significant loans that our three institutions have made to the exhibition, we have benefitted from the long-term loan of early twentieth-century art from the Gianni Mattioli Collection. Laura Mattioli Rossi generously agreed to allow an important Futurist, Umberto Boccioni, to be part of this exhibition. Its loan has been facilitated by Philip Rylands, Director, Peggy Guggenheim Collection, Venice; Paul Schwarzbaum, Chief Conservator, Guggenheim Museums Technical Director, International Projects; and Jasper Sharp, Exhibitions and Collections Coordinator and Chief Registrar.

In preparing the exhibition, we would like to acknowledge the steadfast collaboration and support of Anna Konivets, Senior Research Fellow/Coordinator of the Hermitage-Guggenheim Project; Min Jung Kim, Program Director for Content Alliances of the Guggenheim Museum; and Franz Pichorner, Vice Director of the Kunsthistorisches. Additionally, we are grateful to Nic Iljine, European Representative of the Guggenheim, who has championed this exhibition. At the Guggenheim, Susan Davidson has relied on the invaluable assistance of Ted Mann, Collections Curatorial Assistant, Robin Kaye Goodman, Project Curatorial Assistant, and Tatiana Ceuvas-Guerrara, Hilla Rebay International Fellow. Christine Surtmann at the Kunsthistorisches has lent additional curatorial support. At the Hermitage, we have sought out the expertise of a number of curators in the Western European Department, in particular Boris Asvarisch, Alexander Babin, Mikhail Dedinkin, Ekaterina Deriabina, Natalia Gritsaj, Ludmila Kagane, Elena Karchova, Albert Kostenevich, and Irina Sokolova.

The gifted and dedicated staff of art professionals at our respective institutions have greatly contributed to a smooth undertaking of this project. At the Guggenheim, we would like to thank Marc Steiglitz, Deputy Director for Finance and Operations, and Anthony Calnek, Deputy Director for Communications and Publishing, who have guided every aspect of this exhibition. Brendan Connell, Assistant Legal Council, and Marion Kahan, Exhibition Program Manager, have swiftly conducted the planning aspects of this project. Hannah Blumenthal, Financial Analyst for Museum Affiliates, and Kim Kanatani, Gail Engelberg Director of Museum Education, have overseen the financial and educational programmings of the exhibition. Meryl Cohen, Director of Registration and Art Services, and Mary Louise Napier, Senior Registrar, deftly executed the complex shipping arrangements in association with Olga Ilmenkova, Head of the Loan Agreement Department at the Hermitage, and Ruperta Pichler, Registrar at the Kunsthistorisches. Carolynn Karp and Dan Zuzunaga, Exhibition Design Assistants, contributed significantly to the design of the exhibition. Julie Barten, Conservator, Exhibitions and Administration, Eleanora Nagy, Sculpture Conservator, Gillian MacMillian, Senior Conservator, and Mara Guglielmi, Paper Conservator, at the Guggenheim, and Elke Oberthaler, Head of Paintings Conservation, at the Kunsthistorisches, assisted carefully in the review of each piece's condition. In New York, David Bufano, Chief Preparator, Jeffrey Clemens, Associate Preparator, and Liza Martin, Art Handler, prepared the artworks for shipping, and in Las Vegas, Max Fernando Bensuaski, Project Manager, seamlessly moved and installed them. Mary Ann Hoag, Lighting Designer, has carefully lit the works and David Heald has recorded the installation photographically.

Robert Rosenblum, Nan and Stephen Swid Curator of Twentieth-Century Art at the Guggenheim, has written delightful texts, and we thank him for his cheerful insights into the topic at hand. The publication has benefited from the discriminating attention of Edward Weisberger, Editor, and freelance editors Jennifer Knox White and Rachel Shuman as well as the clear-sighted design of intern Janice Lee in collaboration with Marcia Fardella, Chief Graphic Designer. Christine Sullivan, Graphic Designer, has also contributed to the graphic presentation of the exhibition. Elizabeth Levy, Director of Publications, Elizabeth Franzen, Managing Editor, and Tracy Hennige, Production Assistant, have each offered their guidance and meticulousness in producing the exhibition's catalogue. Our respective photography departments have acted quickly to supply material, and we are thankful to Kim Bush at the Guggenheim, Isle Jung at the Kunsthistorisches, and Xenia Pushnitskaya at the Hermitage.

The Pursuit of Pleasure is hosted by the Guggenheim Hermitage Museum under the managing directorship of Elizabeth Herridge, and her staff, in particular Daniel Sherman, Marketing and Public Relations Manager, have once again paved the way for a successful collaboration. Additionally, we would like to acknowledge the support of the Venetian Resort-Hotel-Casino, in particular Scott J. Messinger, Vice President of Brand Marketing, and Robert McFarland, Art Director.

Susan Davidson
Curator
Solomon R. Guggenheim Museum

Arkady Ippolitov
Curator of Italian Prints
State Hermitage Museum

Karl Schütz
Director, Gemäldegalerie
Kunsthistorisches Museum

The Pursuit of Pleasure

Most museum visitors assume they belong to the very lowest rung of the ladder of art appreciation. What do they know about all those things experts keep talking about—the mysteries of color, line, composition; the arguments about whether a Rembrandt is or isn't a Rembrandt; the ability to distinguish between the great and the mediocre or instantly to classify a work as "Flemish, late sixteenth century"? But I will never forget a succinct counterargument offered by a friend: "There is no wrong way," he declared, "to look at a work of art." Suddenly, a dam seemed to burst, and I realized as never before that there really are endless ways of classifying and enjoying art. After all, art is made by human beings, who themselves are infinitely complicated. Moreover, art can mirror just about anything on this planet or in outer space that we can see or do or feel. There is nothing, it seems, that artists have not depicted, whether a newborn infant or an aging beggar, a bushel of potatoes or a platter of oysters, a blade of grass or a spiral nebula. And there is no emotion that has not been registered, whether desire, remorse, faith, or jubilation. There are infinite ways of shuffling the deck.

I thought about this again in 1996. That year, the Olympic Summer Games were held in Atlanta, Georgia, marking the one-hundredth anniversary of the first revival, in 1896, of this ancient Greek tradition, held, appropriately, in Athens. By 1996, art could also play a part in this celebration. At the High Museum of Art in Atlanta, an exhibition titled *Rings: Five Passions in World Art* joined forces with the games. Culled from all continents and spanning more than seven millennia, the art in this exhibition was organized in a most unfamiliar way. The classifications, in fact, were based on universal human experiences—love, anguish, awe, triumph, and joy—and in each category one could find anything from Hawaiian idols to Harlem jitterbugs, from Peruvian Christian icons to a major Matisse. Such diversity, of course, can be found in many of the world's greatest museums, but it was a tonic jolt to see these works joined in such new combinations. Dealing with primal human emotions, the tone of the exhibition was lofty, but it reminded me that of the countless ways to look at art, none is necessarily more right or wrong than any other.

FIG. I
Michelangelo Merisi da Caravaggio
(Italian, ca. 1571–1610)
The Lute Player, ca. 1595
Oil on canvas
37 x 46 ⅞ inches (94 x 119 cm)
State Hermitage Museum,
St. Petersburg

FIG. 2
Vincent van Gogh (Dutch, 1853–1890)
Night Café, 1888
27 ½ x 35 inches (70 x 88.9 cm)
Oil on canvas
Yale University Art Gallery,
New Haven, Bequest of Stephen Carlton
Clark, B.A. 1903

I was once particularly amused to find myself visiting the art museum in the small Burgundian city of Bourg-en-Bresse, renowned for its plump, thoroughbred chickens, the top of the poultry charts. Lo and behold, the museum had a little section called "La Volaille dans l'Art," or "Poultry in Art." There, in the form of oil paintings, bronzes, and marbles, was a new type of barnyard filled with chickens, ducks, turkeys, and guinea hens, enough to make farmers swell with pride and dinner guests lick their chops. Ever since, when I see, for example, a rooster in a painting, I might think not only of its silly vanity or its symbolism as the Gallic cock, but also of how nicely it would have fit into this display.

Another example: One day, passing by the window of a store that sold supplies for poolrooms, I saw, to my shock, a cheap reproduction of Vincent van Gogh's *Night Café* (1888; fig. 2) hanging on the wall. This world-famous painting features a green baize billiard table dominating an anxiety-ridden space, where a handful of depressed or drunken night owls seem to have been sitting forever. My immediate reaction was that this was an unintentional joke on poor van Gogh, who clearly did not paint his nightmare picture to be used as an advertisement in a New York store. But is this necessarily a "wrong" way to look at the painting? Slowly,

I began to realize that van Gogh's painting could also be related to other, earlier depictions of gaming rooms with pool tables and that such images, whether cheap popular illustrations of the sports of the day or classier oil paintings, might have been part of van Gogh's own image bank, triggering his choice of what would dominate the canvas. And in fact, one such painting can be found here, in the work of an early nineteenth-century French painter, Louis Léopold Boilly (cat. no. 22)—which brings us to the exhibition at hand.

This might be seen as another demonstration of how there are no wrong ways to look at art, an anthology in which many very different artists (from Peter Paul Rubens to Alfred Maurer) who lived in very different centuries (from the sixteenth to the twentieth) and places (from Flanders to the United States) are jostled together, joined by unexpected connections. In this case, the abiding theme—appropriate, it is hoped, to an exhibition in Las Vegas—is given in the title, *The Pursuit of Pleasure*. That, of course, covers a multitude of blessings and sins and an equal variety of ways to have a good time. Cutting across the more enjoyable side of art history with this broad swathe, four groups have emerged. In the first, "Music and Dance," the theme is as old as humankind and will surely go on inspiring artists until the end of time.

FIG. 3
Edgar Degas (French, 1834–1917)
The Rehearsal of the Ballet Onstage, probably 1874
Oil mixed with turpentine, with traces of watercolor and pastel over pen and ink on paper, laid on board and mounted on canvas
21 ⅜ x 28 ¾ inches (54.3 x 73 cm)
The Metropolitan Museum of Art, New York, H.O. Havemeyer Collection, Gift of Horace Havemeyer, 1929

No matter which of the great museums we visit, we find pertinent examples and can hear the sound and feel the beat, whether at the State Hermitage Museum, St. Petersburg, in Caravaggio's sexy teenage lutenist (fig. 1), at the Metropolitan Museum of Art, New York, in Edgar Degas's ballerinas preparing for a performance (fig. 3), or at the Kunsthistorisches Museum, Vienna, in Pieter Bruegel the Elder's wedding festivities (fig. 4).

FIG. 4
Pieter Bruegel the Elder
(Flemish, 1525/30–1569)
Peasant Wedding, ca. 1568–69
Oil on wood
44 ⅞ x 64 ⁹⁄₁₆ inches (114 x 164 cm)
Gemäldegalerie, Kunsthistorisches
Museum, Vienna
1027

In the second group, "Celebration and Café Society," another full gamut is run, embracing everything from 1920s nightclubs and Dutch brothels to Bastille Day festivities in modern Paris and a humble meal shared by Spanish peasants. In the third group, "Gaming and Sport," we discover that artists have chronicled a wide range of fun and games, taking us from a sport that has become more and more of an endangered species—the hunting of wild animals—to the familiar exertions of riding a bicycle or chasing a football. Finally, in the fourth group, the pleasures of the body shift from the athletic to the erotic. "Flirtation and Romance," introduces more intimate pleasures, moving, as it were, from the restaurant to the bedroom. Cupid controls this territory, which includes everything from raucous drunks grasping for girlfriends to frolics in rococo gardens fit for Marie Antoinette. As all of these painters and sculptors show us, there are as many ways to pursue pleasure as there are to look at art.

Catalogue

Music & Dance

Music & Dance

We are so used to hearing music by flicking a switch that we often forget that in other centuries, music meant live music, performed everywhere from churches and opera houses to drawing rooms and brothels. And music, of course, could also belong to the classical gods—a lyre accompanying the recitation of poetry, or pipes and percussion firing the excitement of a revelry dedicated to Bacchus. A charming little reminder of these bacchanals is found in a painting from sixteenth-century Venice, *The Small Tambourine Player* by Titian (cat. no. 1). Here, singled out from mythological territory, is a lone *putto* (the Italian word for a plump infant who, often assuming the role of Cupid, is sure to be found at parties given by Greeks and Romans). With a mischievous smile, this *putto*, perhaps a fragment from a larger painting, seems to be warming up his tambourine before joining the other infant musicians who will keep up the beat at a festival of the gods.

The more earthbound counterparts to these Olympian scenes are particularly abundant in seventeenth-century art, where real-life people, solo or in groups, open their mouths in song and often play musical instruments that we do not quite recognize as ours. In a painting by Bernardo Strozzi, a lute is plucked the way a modern music-maker might strum an electric guitar (cat. no. 3). In a painting by Ferdinand Bol, a young girl confidently holds a *lira de gamba*, the Renaissance ancestor of the modern cello (cat. no. 5). Such instruments give us a sense of time travel to another world, both familiar and strange. Familiar it is, since most of these people, though unnamed, look like individuals made of the same mortal flesh as ours. They twist and turn, laugh and smile, as if their movements and expressions have been captured by a modern camera, like the merry group gathered in Jan Miense Molenaer's *Peasants Playing Music* (mid-17th century; cat. no. 4). But these are paintings of the seventeenth century, which, like movies staged in other decades or centuries, can offer us the surprise of different clothing, different musical scores, and different instruments, and, as in Jan Gerritsz van Bronckhorst's *Merry Society with a Violin Player* (ca. 1640; cat. no. 2), a glimpse of the way music making can lead to the bedroom.

In the twentieth-century paintings in this section, the music keeps playing, but the life portrayed may still seem remote from our own. The musician who fiddles away in Marc Chagall's

Green Violinist (1923–24; cat. no. 9) wafts us not only to a fairy-tale world where human skin can be green and people and farm animals can fly through the air with the greatest of ease, but also to the memory of a Russian shtetl, the kind of segregated Jewish community in which the artist was born as well as the cultural origin of Sholem Aleichem's legendary stories and *Fiddler on the Roof*. The setting of Félix Vallotton's *Woman at a Piano* (1904; cat. no. 7)—the parlor of a country house whose open French windows bring the sunlight and burgeoning landscape indoors—may well make us feel at home. But somehow the isolated lady playing the piano for no one but herself evokes a nineteenth-century intimacy, for it was then common, as in earlier centuries, for women to learn musical skills that could add to the domestic pleasures of a lonely morning or, as a more communal diversion, entertain a house filled with guests.

As in a Titian bacchanal, music and dance are inseparable (a point made unforgettably in the State Hermitage Museum's famous duo by Henri Matisse, *Music* and *Dance* of 1910). In *The Pursuit of Pleasure*, we have two modern dancers, one in two dimensions and the other in three, who almost make us hear the musical rhythms that inspire their movements. With her fiery lipstick and her orange-red skirt billowing in a wild cancan, Kees van Dongen's cabaret dancer of 1907 (cat. no. 8) looks like a still from the movie *Moulin Rouge*, her brash colors and gestures instantly conjuring up the giddiest pleasures of nightlife during the Belle Epoque. Edgar Degas's little bronze is another matter, here we can almost hear the dancer's castanets clicking in tandem with her perfectly poised body (cat. no. 6).

Pablo Picasso's uncannily animated *Mandolin and Guitar* (1924; cat. no. 10) offers an unexpected mixture of music and dance on a tabletop. A master of metamorphosis, Picasso often made his still-life objects look alive, even humanoid, and in this sumptuous painting, the guitar, that symbol of Spain, stands as erect as the guitarist who would play it, vibrating in a rhythm caught by the supine mandolin, as if they were a pair of lovers. Between them, the upright bottle of red wine does its own little dance, its wriggling contours so contagious that the three apples below seem to bob up and down with the beat. Seldom has a still life been less still, or a mute painting so full of imaginary sounds.

I. **Titian (Tiziano Vecellio)** (Italian, 1488–1576)
The Small Tambourine Player, ca. 1550
Oil on canvas
22 ⅝ x 20 ½ inches (57.5 x 52 cm)
Gemäldegalerie, Kunsthistorisches Museum, Vienna
96

2. **Jan Gerritsz van Bronckhorst** (Dutch, 1603–1661)
Merry Society with a Violin Player, ca. 1640
Oil on canvas
47 ¼ x 58 ¼ inches (120 x 148 cm)
State Hermitage Museum, St. Petersburg
3303

3. **Bernardo Strozzi** (Italian, 1518–1644)
Lute Player, 1640–44
Oil on canvas
36 ¼ x 29 ¹⁵⁄₁₆ inches (92 x 76 cm)
Gemäldegalerie, Kunsthistorisches Museum, Vienna
1612

4. **Jan Miense Molenaer** (Flemish, 1609–1668)
Peasants Playing Music, mid-17th century
Oil on wood
20 ⅞ x 20 ½ inches (53 x 52 cm)
Gemäldegalerie, Kunsthistorisches Museum, Vienna
5909

5. **Ferdinand Bol** (Dutch, 1616–1680)
Girl with Lira de Gamba, 1653
Oil on canvas
43 11⁄16 x 34 ¼ inches (111 x 87 cm)
Gemäldegalerie, Kunsthistorisches Museum, Vienna
9050

6. **Edgar Degas** (French, 1834–1917)
Spanish Dance, 1896–1911
Bronze
15 ⅞ x 6 ½ x 7 inches (40.3 x 16.5 x 17.8 cm)
Solomon R. Guggenheim Museum, New York,
Thannhauser Collection, Gift, Justin K. Thannhauser
78.2514.9

7. **Félix Vallotton** (French, 1865–1925)
Woman at a Piano, 1904
Oil on canvas
17 ⅛ x 22 ⁷⁄₁₆ inches (43.5 x 57 cm)
State Hermitage Museum, St. Petersburg
4860

8. **Kees van Dongen** (Dutch, 1877–1968)
Red Dancer, 1907
Oil on canvas
35 ¹³⁄₁₆ x 31 ⅞ inches (91 x 81cm)
State Hermitage Museum, St. Petersburg
9129

10. **Pablo Picasso** (Spanish, 1881–1973)
Mandolin and Guitar, 1924
Oil with sand on canvas
55 ⅜ x 78 ⅞ inches (140.7 x 200.3 cm)
Solomon R. Guggenheim Museum, New York
53.1358

Celebration & Café Society

Celebration & Café Society

People can convene to declare war, pray in church, or attend school, but the ones in this group of works, whether lowly seventeenth-century peasants or well-heeled Parisian ladies from 1900, are getting together to have a good time. As for the peasants, we expect them to be rowdy, whether having a simple meal or celebrating a wedding. In Diego Rodríguez de Silva y Velázquez's *Luncheon* (ca. 1617–18; cat. no. 11), we are thrust right into the near end of a table where a trio of men, one from each of the traditional three stages of life (junior, grown-up, and senior), seem to be inviting us to drink their wine, grab their loaf of bread, peel their two pomegranates, and try their mussels. The knife protruding in the extreme foreground becomes a virtual invitation for a new guest. A raised wine glass, a big youthful smile, and a "thumbs up" counter the old man's sobriety, beckoning us to enjoy this modest meal in good company.

The pleasures of alcohol are as timeless in art as in human history, and in this show we discover that even monks of centuries past were hardly teetotalers. In Eduard von Grützner's *Visit to Monks* (ca. 1900; cat. no. 13), we have a perfect example of a humorous theme much favored by nineteenth-century audiences—namely, behind-the-scenes views of members of the clergy pursuing pleasure when nobody is looking, gorging themselves on food and drink. Here we descend to a dank cellar, not to meditate with the monks on the afterlife, but to watch them enjoying another round of drinks during a pause from their more pious duties. In fact, they turn this holy ground into what looks more like a *Ratskeller* than a monastery.

Alcohol appears to be the theme in *The Soldier Drinks* (1911–12; cat. no. 17), Marc Chagall's recollection, during his first visit to Paris, of his childhood past in Vitebsk, where, during the Russo-Japanese War of 1904–05, soldiers were often housed in private homes. Many commentators have thought that this soldier is tipsy (his military cap floats dizzily above his head), but the artist himself denied this reading. The soldier, after all, is holding his cup under a samovar, drinking tea, not vodka, even though, as usual, Chagall's magical colors and dislocating shifts of scale, from huge (the soldier) to tiny (the happy lovers in the foreground), seem to intoxicate the entire painting.

More measured and more public entertainments are found in this grouping, too. Dirck Hals, Frans's less famous brother, opens a vista onto the courtliest of garden parties, where a ceremonial decorum reigns (cat. no. 12). Like their greyhounds, the guests evoke high breeding, exercising the restraint demanded by their ritual gestures of polite conversation and courtship, not to mention by their extravagant clothing, which hampers natural movement.

This vision of elegant ladies and gentlemen enjoying the pleasures of nature is surprisingly brought up to date in Vasily Kandinsky's *Pastorale* (1911; cat. no. 16). At first glance, this looks like one of his adventurous early works in which floods of molten color dissolve the visible, material world. But at second glance, we realize that this fluid rainbow actually camouflages a fairy-tale scene in which we slowly discern people, animals, and landscape. The smudges of purplish red in the upper right-hand corner turn out to be rouge on the cheeks of three women in nineteenth-century period costume, courtly ladies who, bearing flowers and accompanied by a top-hatted gentleman, step into an enchanted country idyll where farm animals roam and graze.

Kandinsky's evocation of long-ago pleasures is a far cry from the glimpses of modern urban entertainment offered here by three foreign artists in Paris. In a Degas-like overhead view of a Parisian café painted in 1905 by Alfred Maurer, a gifted young American member of the Gertrude Stein circle, propriety reigns within a regimented order (cat. no. 15). Rectangular tables covered with white tablecloths, in tandem with the curved backs and seats of the Thonet chairs, impose, at an oblique angle, a perfect grid over the café and its clients. Whether alone or in twos or threes, these customers do nothing to disturb the pattern, their backs upright, their hats in perfect place.

A different kind of formality prevails in the German painter Max Beckmann's view of Parisian society in 1931 (cat. no. 18). This cramped gathering of men and women in evening attire, with the cheek-by-jowl jostling of tuxedos, bared shoulders, beaked noses, and self-satisfied grimaces, offers a caricatural cross section of the rich and famous that almost reads as an indictment of a smug, privileged group who barely deign to look down at us. Thirty years earlier, in 1901, another foreigner in Paris, the Spaniard Pablo Picasso, offered a very different, populist slice of society, captured on the national holiday Bastille Day (cat. no. 14). His painted souvenir seizes the pleasurable confusion of the anonymous, often faceless Parisian crowds who mill about and dance with joy, becoming part of what looks like an Impressionist painting that, as if lit by a firecracker, detonates an explosion of sputtering, patriotic colors.

II. **Diego Rodríguez de Silva y Velázquez** (Spanish, 1599–1660)
Luncheon, ca. 1617–18
Oil on canvas
42 ¹¹⁄₁₆ x 40 ³⁄₁₆ inches (108.5 x 102 cm)
State Hermitage Museum, St. Petersburg
520

12. **Dirck Hals** (Dutch, 1591–1656)
Garden Stroll, ca. 1632
Oil on wood
12 ³⁄₁₆ x 20 ¼ inches (31 x 51.5 cm)
Gemäldegalerie, Kunsthistorisches Museum, Vienna
6083

13. **Eduard von Grützner** (German, 1846–1925)
   Visit to Monks, ca. 1900
   Oil on canvas
   39 ⅜ x 35 inches (100 x 89 cm)
   State Hermitage Museum, St. Petersburg
   9094

14. **Pablo Picasso** (Spanish, 1881–1973)
The Fourteenth of July, 1901
Oil on cardboard, mounted on canvas
18 ⅞ x 24 ¾ inches (47.9 x 62.9 cm)
Solomon R. Guggenheim Museum, New York,
Thannhauser Collection, Gift, Justin K. Thannhauser
78.2514.36

15. **Alfred Maurer** (American, 1868–1932)
In a Café, 1905
Oil on cardboard
35 7/16 x 31 5/16 inches (90 x 79.5 cm)
State Hermitage Museum, St. Petersburg
8919

16. **Vasily Kandinsky** (Russian, 1866–1944)
Pastorale, February 1911
Oil on canvas
41 ⅝ x 61 ⅝ inches (105.7 x 156.5 cm)
Solomon R. Guggenheim Museum, New York
45.965

17. **Marc Chagall** (Belarussian, 1887–1985)
The Soldier Drinks, 1911–12
Oil on canvas
43 x 37 ¼ inches (109.2 x 94.6 cm)
Solomon R. Guggenheim Museum, New York
49.1211

18. **Max Beckmann** (German, 1884–1950)
   Paris Society, 1931
   Oil on canvas
   43 x 69 ⅛ inches (109.2 x 175.6 cm)
   Solomon R. Guggenheim Museum, New York
   70.1927

Gaming & Sport

Gaming & Sport

Hunting animals for food may be as prehistoric as love making, but it took many centuries for it to become not only a means of survival, but also a part of a repertory of pleasurable entertainment for those who already had quite enough for dinner. European monarchs were so addicted to hunting that many of them, including Charles I of England and Philip IV of Spain, hired the greatest painters to immortalize them in their hunting garb, accompanied by their rifles, horses, and hounds. And this kind of blood sport, still flourishing today among the British aristocracy, also penetrated less lofty layers of society. A Dutch seventeenth-century painting by Philips Wouwerman offers the spectacle of a group of elegantly dressed huntsmen, falcons in hand, preparing to set off into the forest as the hunting horn is sounded and the sky darkens with the threat of a storm that may add extra excitement to the chase (cat. no. 21).

To be sure, most hunting scenes from the Middle Ages through the nineteenth century involved local fauna—the usual quail and pheasant, boar and deer, wolf and fox—but often they included stronger, more exotic combats, occasionally even with wild animals whose natural habitat was far from Europe. Peter Paul Rubens, for example, depicted lion and tiger hunts that look Western but take place in the Arab world. And at times, as in an extraordinarily precocious canvas of 1722 by Phillip Ferdinand de Hamilton, a little-known Dutch painter who specialized in animals, man the hunter is entirely banished from the scene (cat. no. 20). Here, we are left with a savage dog-eat-dog combat in a distant, exotic world, where a ferocious leopard, while seizing its feathered victim, is suddenly interrupted by a hideous vulture that is after the same meal.

Images of fierce animals and malevolent nature were, in fact, more familiar to Romantic artists of the early nineteenth century, as in Eugène Delacroix's heated vision of two Moroccans who, crouching and hiding like wild animals, ambush a roaring lion (cat. no. 24). Painted in 1854, Delacroix's hunting scene continues to evoke the artist's memory of a voyage taken some twenty years earlier to North Africa, where he felt immersed in a world light-years away from modern Europe, a world thrillingly close to the lair of the beast.

Needless to say, most sports and games were considerably less life threatening, and while some artists depicted the kind of exotic combats we enjoy today on such TV programs as *The Crocodile Hunter*, most of them were content to render more-domesticated indoor and outdoor games. Painters in seventeenth-century Holland were particularly eager to turn out agreeable images of the nation at play. Hendrick Avercamp, a specialist in winter skating rinks, is represented here by a characteristic canvas that offers us an overhead view of cheerful folk who, framed by snow-covered, leafless trees, seem to be having so much fun that many of these amateurs actually manage to dance on ice, a casual preview of a contemporary sport usually practiced by highly skilled professionals (cat. no. 19).

For those daunted by chilly weather, there was always a card game available, a subject that flourished in seventeenth-century painting, both north and south of the Alps. Card games permitted artists to explore all kinds of psychological intrigue, from the habits of thieves and wily gamblers to the grimacing expressions of those who win or lose. In his painting here, the Flemish master Theodoor Rombouts seizes a characteristic moment among card players, when, like kibitzers, we watch the tense and quiet drama of one of the most universally popular games (cat. no. 23).

Many of these indoor or outdoor entertainments may look remote to contemporary eyes, but this section also includes a group of paintings from the nineteenth and twentieth centuries that should make us feel more at home. It is easy to connect with the painting by Louis Léopold Boilly, which gives us an angled view of a game of billiards as played in Paris in 1807 (cat. no. 22). We may immediately associate this with the pool tables in our own bars (although, in fact, billiards is a somewhat different game from pool), but what is surprising is the wide spectrum of Parisians who unwind in this communal space. Wearing the simple, antique-inspired white dresses so fashionable during the Napoleonic Empire, women are conspicuous in a scene we associate with men. One of them, viewed seductively from behind, is an active player, displaying her sexy contours under a clinging dress, but many of them are just there to enjoy the get-together, which includes nursing mothers and an assortment of playful children and dogs. Onlookers enjoy cups of coffee on the left, while personal intrigues between ladies and gentlemen can be observed here and there. For a billiards parlor, all seems harmonious, a leisurely cross section of Parisian society having a good time under the pleasant, natural illumination of a skylight.

We can also recognize in this section, though through far more distorted lenses, other images of sports familiar to our time. Charmingly offbeat, a picture of football players by the famous self-taught "primitive" painter Henri Rousseau is a delight in its childlike efforts to depict four men in striped uniforms going after a ball that, like the Moon, seems eternally suspended (cat. no. 25). Despite the title, *The Football Players*, the game is not, in fact, football, but rugby, which was just becoming a fad in France in 1908, the date of Rousseau's canvas. As such, *The Football Players* is a harbinger of a whole run of early twentieth-century paintings of what the French call *la vie sportive* (the sporting life), which, inspired by memories of the Olympic Games, was to promote discipline and health for all the people of France.

Even across the Rhine, artists like Paul Klee absorbed modern competitive sports into their fantastic universe. His 1921 watercolor *Runner at the Goal* (cat. no. 27) may well have been inspired by a race the artist witnessed in Germany, but it also represents the dream of every child who wishes, with outstretched leg, to reach the goal before the others do and who is rewarded by being number one, a prize Klee conspicuously inscribed on the runner's forehead.

Inevitably, twentieth-century artists also turned their attention to the mechanized sports launched by a new, motorized world of automobiles and airplanes. Nowhere did the excitement of this conquest of speed and energy reach higher levels than in the work of the youthful and rebellious Italian Futurists on the eve of World War I. Eager to embrace every new technology, they charged their artistic batteries with spinning wheels and metallic parts. A perfect example here is Umberto Boccioni's *Dynamism of a Cyclist* (1913; cat. no. 26), in which the cyclist and his bicycle seem to be morphed into a hybrid man-machine of such breathtaking velocity that we feel the mirage will be gone in the blink of an eye. Part of a new world of motorcycles and the Tour de France, it looks as fresh as ever. As we all know today, pleasure can be pursued even on the highways.

19. **Hendrick Avercamp** (Dutch, 1585–1634)
Winter Landscape, ca. 1605
Oil on panel
11 ⅝ x 18 ¼ inches (29.5 x 46.4 cm)
Gemäldegalerie, Kunsthistorisches Museum, Vienna
5659

20. **Phillip Ferdinand de Hamilton** (Dutch, 1667–1750)
Leopard and Hawk, 1722
Oil on canvas
34 ⅜ x 47 ¼ inches (88 x 120 cm)
Gemäldegalerie, Kunsthistorisches Museum, Vienna
382

21. **Philips Wouwerman** (Dutch, 1619–1668)
Huntsmen Setting Out, mid-17th century
Oil on canvas
21 ⅝ x 31 ½ inches (55 x 80 cm)
State Hermitage Museum, St. Petersburg
836

23. **Theodoor Rombouts** (Flemish, 1597–1637)
   Card Playing, first quarter of 17th century
   Oil on canvas
   56 ⁵⁄₁₆ x 88 inches (143 x 223.5 cm)
   State Hermitage Museum, St. Petersburg
   522

24. **Eugène Delacroix** (French, 1798–1863)
Lion Hunting in Morocco, 1854
Oil on canvas
29 ⅛ x 36 ¼ inches (74 x 92 cm)
State Hermitage Museum, St. Petersburg
3853

25. **Henri Rousseau** (French, 1844–1910)
The Football Players, 1908
Oil on canvas
39 ½ x 31 ⅝ inches (100.3 x 80.3 cm)
Solomon R. Guggenheim Museum, New York
60.1583

26. **Umberto Boccioni** (Italian, 1882–1916)
Dynamism of a Cyclist, 1913
Oil on canvas
27 9/16 x 37 3/8 inches (70 x 95 cm)
Gianni Mattioli Collection, On long-term loan to
the Peggy Guggenheim Collection, Venice

27. **Paul Klee** (Swiss, 1879–1940)
Runner at the Goal, 1921
Watercolor and pencil on paper, mounted on cardboard with gouache
15 ½ x 11 ⅞ inches (39.4 x 30.2 cm) overall
Solomon R. Guggenheim Museum, New York
48.1172.55

Flirtation & Romance

Flirtation & Romance

*A*mour, *amor, amore, Liebe.* It is no surprise that love, which makes the world go round, has always dominated art. In the works shown in this section, it comes in countless varieties, sometimes from the great, remote tales of history and literature and sometimes from more modern practices of seduction, which can range from the bawdy to the refined. We find here the legendary femme fatale Cleopatra, as painted by Jacob Jordaens, a Flemish master who, like his contemporary Peter Paul Rubens, enjoyed painting the pleasures of ruddy, zaftig flesh (cat. no. 31). This Cleopatra, in fact, looks less like an Egyptian queen than a reveler in an Antwerp tavern, centuries away from the Nile. The scene depicts an often-told tale of how Cleopatra, at a banquet, again proved her wanton extravagance by dissolving a precious pearl in a glass of vinegar and then drinking it down.

We also find here the most famous of lovers, Shakespeare's star-crossed Romeo and Juliet, a totally different version of love's blind passion (cat. no. 38). As imagined by the most famous sculptor of the nineteenth century, Auguste Rodin, this is a surprisingly carnal interpretation of the tragic pair, closer to the artist's frequent representations of a primal embrace by anonymous Adams and Eves.

Chronologically, this section takes us first to less high-minded territory, the bar down the street. By 1600, tavern and brothel scenes had begun to flourish in Northern Europe, especially in seventeenth-century Flanders and Holland, where one painting after another evoked after-hours pleasures. The theme of this section is perfectly introduced in a turn-of-the-century painting by the much-traveled German painter Hans von Aachen, who, like so many of his contemporaries, discovered that not only the loves of the gods, but also those of the coarsest, most drunken contemporary couples were quite enough to make an enjoyable picture. The lively pair in his *Joking Couple* (ca. 1596; cat. no. 28), a close-up from the corner of some tavern, is so convulsed in laughter that we can almost hear the cackling. And we can also imagine the next step, which in many other paintings is couched in biblical or moralizing guise. So it is that a Dutch painter, Johannes Baeck, in *Parable of the Prodigal Son* (1637; cat. no. 30), seems to use the Old Testament legend as an excuse for raising the curtain on a scene of cheerful debauchery in which musicians (including a woman playing the *lira da gamba*, also seen in Ferdinand Bol's painting [cat. no. 5]) provide a seductive background for the smirking encounter between the profligate son and a local, bare-breasted whore. We can hardly remember the remorseful conclusion of the biblical story, especially since these players are wearing contemporary clothing.

The same kind of trick is played in another Dutch painting, Jan Steen's *In Luxury Beware* (1663; cat. no. 32), in which a lesson in good household behavior becomes the pretext for an entertaining and often lewd display of the world upside down. Everything is wrong in this home: a little boy is already smoking; the family's pet spaniel is on the table eating a meat pie; and less-domesticated animals have invaded the premises. A monkey plays with the clock on the wall; a pig eats scraps off the floor; and a duck settles on somebody's shoulder. Center stage and most outrageous to domestic decorum, the head of the family carouses with a whore who, her own legs separated, holds a wine glass between his open legs, while his wife snoozes through it all. Their behavior presumably teaches us what not to do, but it also tells us how much fun can be had, especially for the father, when things run amok. An artist from a later century, Henri de Toulouse-Lautrec, would get right to the point. His view of a brothel parlor, *In the Salon* (1893; cat. no. 36), is matter-of-fact enough to offer documentation for a history of the sex trade in turn-of-the-century Paris.

But love and sex can also be wafted off to Arcadian lands, as in Rubens's fertile and benevolent *Landscape with Rainbow* (ca. 1632–35; cat. no. 29). The amorous figures who inhabit this Flemish

Garden of Eden may be peasants, but their ancestry almost seems mythological. Couples join in graceful poses, a shepherd pipes his pipe, sheep quietly graze, and all of nature, from the lush grass and trees to the distant hills, is blessed with a double rainbow. This is surely the land of milk and honey.

A similar mix of past and present pervades Jean-Baptiste Pater's early eighteenth-century glimpse of presumably contemporary women (some still wearing their time-bound clothing) who, without a man in sight—except, of course, for the viewer—enjoy the pleasures of bathing in natural waters (cat. no. 33). At the left, a marble statue of Venus reclining on a huge seashell, accompanied by a bare-bottomed Cupid, clearly sets the mythic mood, as if Diana and her bathing nymphs had suddenly been transformed into eighteenth-century fantasies of erotic freedom. The mood of dreamlike pleasure also radiates from another French eighteenth-century painting, this one by Nicolas Lancret. In *The Swing* (1730s; cat. no. 34), we see a courtship ritual familiar in French art before the Revolution—namely, the symbolic seduction of a young lady by a suitor who, in a fragile landscape, more imagined than real, joins her in the foreplay of a rhythmic thrust that swings her back and forth under a tree. The relaxed audience of other would-be couples turns this playful country outing into an imaginary Garden of Love.

And love is also the engine behind a painting by a more famous French eighteenth-century master, Jean-Honoré Fragonard (cat. no. 35). This time, the setting is distinctly humble, more of a servants' quarter than an enchanted forest. The still-innocent teenage country girl has been suddenly grasped by the shoulder and kissed by an equally young boy, while her girlfriend acts as an accomplice, holding her friend's right hand and wrist as if taking her amorous pulse. Sexual awakening has seldom been couched in such a gently playful, pillow-soft language.

This youthful initiate is a far cry from the more professional intimacy with women's love lives depicted in Edouard Manet's *Before the Mirror*, painted in 1876, the heyday of Impressionism (cat. no. 37). Here again we become Peeping Toms, but this time we stealthily watch from behind, like intruders in a lady's boudoir. What we see is her back, not her face, a combination of fully bared shoulders and the painful restraints of a corset that she seems to be adjusting. The seemingly anonymous, faceless lady has in fact been convincingly identified as Henriette Hauser, a famous courtesan who, among her other triumphs, was the mistress of the Prince of Orange. But more important for Manet and for us is the dazzle and mystery of the image in the cheval glass, which seems to absorb the figure into its icy shimmer, rendered with a tour de force of what look like recklessly slashing brushstrokes. This image of feminine vanity, the intimate preparation for the next encounter, harks back, like so many of these views of contemporary life, to mythological sources. Not surprisingly, the reference here is to the many Old Master paintings of Venus admiring her own beauty in a mirror. Appropriately, the goddess of love continues to reign over all the works in this group.

28. **Hans von Aachen** (German, 1552–1615)
Joking Couple (Self-Portrait with the Artist's Wife), ca. 1596
Oil on canvas
24 ⅞ x 19 ¹¹⁄₁₆ inches (63 x 50 cm)
Gemäldegalerie, Kunsthistorisches Museum, Vienna
1134

29. **Peter Paul Rubens** (Flemish, 1577–1640)
Landscape with Rainbow, ca. 1632–35
Oil on canvas, transferred from panel
33 ⅞ x 50 ³⁄₆ inches (86 x 130 cm)
State Hermitage Museum, St. Petersburg
520

30. **Johannes Baeck** (Dutch, 1610–1654)
Parable of the Prodigal Son, 1637
Oil on canvas
48 ¼ x 72 ⁷⁄₁₆ inches (122.5 x 184 cm)
Gemäldegalerie, Kunsthistorisches Museum, Vienna
7024

31. **Jacob Jordaens** (Flemish, 1593–1678)
The Banquet of Cleopatra, 1653
Oil on canvas
61 ⁹⁄₁₆ x 58 ¾ inches (156.4 x 149.3 cm)
State Hermitage Museum, St. Petersburg
8536

32. **Jan Steen** (Dutch, 1626–1679)
In Luxury Beware, 1663
Oil on canvas
41 5/16 x 57 1/16 inches (105 x 145 cm)
Gemäldegalerie, Kunsthistorisches Museum, Vienna
791

33. **Jean-Baptiste Pater** (French, 1695–1736)
Women Bathing, first half of 18th century
Oil on canvas
29 ½ x 23 ¹³/₁₆ inches (75 x 60.5 cm)
State Hermitage Museum, St. Petersburg
7670

34. **Nicolas Lancret** (French, 1690–1743)
The Swing, 1730s
Oil on canvas
39 x 51 ¹⁵⁄₁₆ inches (99 x 132 cm)
State Hermitage Museum, St. Petersburg
7496

35. **Jean-Honoré Fragonard** (French, 1732–1806)
The Captured Kiss, second half of 18th century
Oil on canvas
18 ½ x 23 ⅝ inches (47 x 60 cm)
State Hermitage Museum, St. Petersburg
5646

36. **Henri de Toulouse-Lautrec** (French, 1864–1901)
In the Salon, 1893
Pastel, gouache, oil, pencil, and watercolor on cardboard
20 ⅞ x 31 ⅜ inches (53 x 79.7 cm)
Solomon R. Guggenheim Museum, New York,
Thannhauser Collection, Gift, Justin K. Thannhauser
78.2514.73

37. **Edouard Manet** (French, 1832–1883)
Before the Mirror, 1876
Oil on canvas
36 ¼ x 28 ⅛ inches (92.1 x 71.4 cm)
Solomon R. Guggenheim Museum, New York,
Thannhauser Collection, Gift, Justin K. Thannhauser
78.2514.27

38. **Auguste Rodin** (French, 1840–1917)
   Romeo and Juliet, 1905
   Marble
   27 $^{15}/_{16}$ inches (71 cm) high
   State Hermitage Museum, St. Petersburg
   1300